FACIN(S

Facing Demons

ANN ALEXANDER

For Sylvia
with best wishes
Ann Alexander

PETERLOO POETS

First published in 2002
by Peterloo Poets
The Old Chapel, Sand Lane, Calstock, Cornwall PL18 9QX, U.K.

**A catalogue record for this book is available
from the British Library**

ISBN   1-871471-21-4

Printed in Great Britain by
Antony Rowe Ltd, Chippenham, Wilts.

ACKNOWLEDGEMENTS

"The Man who is out there" won The Frogmore Prize, 2000.

"The way to the top" was a prizewinner in *The Spectator*, 2000.

"Four women wed" won Third Prize in the Peterloo Open Poetry Competition, 2001.

southwest arts

Contents

Page

9   Respectability costs

10   The Journalist

11   In Africa

12   The Obituary

13   A murderer's wedding day

14   Proper Cornish

16   Didn't hurt

17   During and afterwards

18   Madron

20   Indifference Day

21   Neighbours

22   The copywriter

23   Colonialism

24   Alter ego

25   No Bowl of Cherries

26   Obeying orders

28   The box in a box

29   The man who is out there

30   On Gibbet Hill

31   Now what?

32   A fly did it

33   The winner

34   Holiday snaps

35   The Old Bitch Bites

36   Stuff Science

37   In-flight Disaster

38   Four women wed

40   UFO

41   Generation gap

42   In praise of global warming

43   A red rag to a bull

44   The Cold Shoulder

45   Relationship

46   Joining the Women's Club

47 Word association
48 The Tiger Mother
49 The way to the top
50 Heredity
51 Optimist
52 To a Nightingale
53 In the beginning
54 This is the end of the line, here
55 Remarriage
56 At the conference
57 Unlucky in love
58 Plenty more where that came from
59 Bones
60 The muse
61 she-mails
62 Cutting to the bone
63 The sea at night
64 You'll know him when you see him
65 Failure
66 When the time comes
67 Dead cat poem
68 Blood transfusion
69 It isn't for the sex
70 The exile longs for home
71 I like the stone age best
72 Taken to the Cleaners
73 Letting the anger out
74 This is a house where something died
75 Christening
76 Like I did. Like you will.
78 Rolling in dead things
79 The Scientist
80 A car led the way

Respectability costs

When you're a pillar of society, you can't be seen
smoking dope, dragging on a spliff the size
of a fat cigar, snorting coke.

When you're respectable, you can't
neck a skinful, reel through town,
then spew it all up in Barclay's doorway.

Nice women don't pick up men half their age,
tattoo themselves, have their navels pierced.
They don't shag all day in a rank bed. Nor

Do they drop six kids, live courtesy of the DSS,
spend their benefit on scratch cards and
pig out on pie and chips.

O my dearest, learn from my mistakes.
Don't be respectable.

The Journalist

Stand here with me, on the edge,
the better to observe.
It's safer here. Look: see them begin?
They're bringing the whole lot down.

Back now, stand further back.
Detachment is required, and calm.
There's tremendous power in the falling,
though it seems to come
so silently, so slowly down.

An old Roman, in his villa in Gaul
wrote home: *the peaches are good this year
but oh, the Goths are everywhere.*
He thought himself safe, there on the edge
of the known, the civilized world.

Even so, it's thrilling, because now you see
vistas of sky where there was no sky.
Then mushroom clouds of dust, rising up
blotting out the sun. And there,
look down: a field of rubble,
a wall with bath attached, a door,
someone's wallpaper, a doll.

In Africa

In a mud hut in Africa
a ragged, hungry boy sat down.

Though there was no reason why
or how it could be so, just then
a Sony digital set appeared
on the dusty floor. With Sky.

In spite of the lack of power or plug,
he switched it on. It worked just fine.
The boy's dark eyes in his haunted face
gazed in awe at the curious race

Strutting their stuff before his eyes
with angry faces, brutal cries;
those pig-fat people, stuffing down
strange food, beneath their sullen skies.

My word, he said, *The world out there
beyond my warring, starving plain
has customs that would make me laugh
if I didn't feel so much hunger and pain.*

He cried to his own, his personal God,
and the awful vision passed away:
*Thank you, sprit of the trees —
that I am not as one of these.*

The Obituary

When you read about his life,
that kindly, half-blind précis;
four hundred weasel words, on
the easy passage through the famous school,
the glittering career,
his wit and wisdom, how he was
so admired, by other men,

And at the very end you read
In 1953 he married Muriel,
one daughter, and one son survive –

Oh, Muriel, his true and loving wife,
what was your contribution to this life?

History should record:
In 1953 he was
rescued by a woman, who
in spite of all his triumphs
saw potential in him, nursed him through
his self-doubt, all those infidelities,
the endless drinking bouts, persuaded him
he could make something of himself.
Stand up, girl – take a bow!

Don't hold your breath, Muriel.

A murderer's wedding day

Love, honour, maybe; never obey –
not for him, who never did,
in all the homes and schools and corners
they trapped him in.

No presents. No future.
Still, something worth recording here,
that he, so caged,
should shackle himself yet more.
That he, so beyond the law,
should seek legality.

Why did I do it? Everyone asks that.
Simple. Like finding a trapped fox,
and believing you have the key.

No snaps, no flowers, no virgin white –
not in this hard, rocky place. The handcuff
rings his wrist. The screws joke:
What's a wedding without a screw?

We smile, for they are chained,
and guilty too. We kiss,
chastely, denying their prurient pleasure.
Our thrill is in the thwarting.

Desire is a fairground ride, gone mad,
flinging me here. In his eyes I see
shadows of that other she. In my mouth,
the words I cannot say: *Why did you do it? How?*
Everyone asks him that.

Proper Cornish

The Antiques Roadshow came to town,
and all the locals queued in line
clutching their Cornishness.

The first one was a blatant fake.
Sorry, my handsome, lover, queen,
it's worthless. Look at this mark here —
made in Birmingham. See? Wrong shape,
and plated. Still, nice try, maid. Next.

This was interesting, but just
as phony, and the experts knew
it was an alloy, mix of Wales
and Timbuctoo. *Alas, my bird,*
you just won't do.

The third too scrumpy.
The fourth too duchy.
The fifth too cromlech.
The sixth too pasty.

The seventh one made them stop and stare.
They gathered round. Excitement grew.
The little book that lists each make
and style and mark since Cornishmen
began (around AD eight-ten)
confirmed their hopes. They weighed it,
tested with the tongue (the slightest taste
detects impurity), and then
someone dressed like Ku Klux Klan,
with fake Victorian Druid crown,
called for silence.

        This young man
is pure and perfect! he pronounced.
They cheered the owner, long and loud.
He felt so proud! A tried and tested, guaranteed
pure and perfect Cornish man!
He stood there, grinning, soaking up
the experts' chat of pedigree,
his date of birth, of this and that –
but all the while he really ached
to know what this great thing was worth,
so he could sell it, dreckly, to
some poor tuss living near St Erth.

Didn't hurt

I remember the moment when
I gave up hitting my child.

She was two years old.
She was roaring wild.
It was midnight, toad cold,

And oh, I was desperate. Aching tired,
though tired is hardly the word
for the flaking
disintegrating state I was in.

If you don't shut up, I said,
I'll give you a smack.
She didn't. I did. Crack.

She wouldn't cry. There were no tears.
Instead she looked at me as if
I were her bitter foe. She said:
Didn't hurt.

So I hit her again, only harder.
Still no tears. Her eyes stretched wide.
Didn't hurt, she cried.

Her little voice, so small, so tough
stopped my raised hand. Enough.
I saw the future; endless blows,
endless defiance down the years.
The hitting and hating, hands and words.

It hurt. I wept.
I asked forgiveness, and she slept.

During and afterwards

You think you can't get closer
without crawling into her skin,
but here you are in the act of love,
melted and melded.

Afterwards, you slip apart
wetly in the great bed. Mind
wandering off in unromantic haste
to necessary concerns. You pay the
dues, the lover's courtesies, lie still
awhile, arm beneath neck – already
aching to be free of the weight of her.

Then abruptly off, jack-knife from the
suffocating softness,
back turned to her rumpled need.
Wipe her off with a tissue, arm yourself
in trousers, shirt and coat; throw goodbyes
on the bed like change.

Madron

The village is wild, God knows,
a sulk of cottages, barns, estate;
the kind of mildewed, surly place
with too many mentions in the local rag,
on the crime page.

Beyond the village is a wood,
and deep in the wood a chapel. Built
for a foreign saint, who turned up here
from over there, and set about
taming the locals. Quaint.

A tiny, ruined, granite hut.
A holy place, where fourteen
hundred years of prayer
hang on the grass like mist. Inside,
a ferny altar, crystal spring.
You'll like it there –

But walk on down the muddy path
through the tangled wood;
go further where the brambles tear
and branches clutch at clothes and hair;
cut through alien plants, and go
places where you shouldn't – there

You'll find a shrivelled, stunted tree.

At first you'll think it's spring, come late.
A hundred different strips of rag
are tied to that tree, along with notes
in a plastic bag, telling of sickness, love, or need;
reeking of lust, or spite, or greed.

Some put there just a while ago
by those whose fast retreating feet
echo still on the woodland floor.

Fresh offerings to an older God,
there a thousand years before
the foreign saint, in the granite hut
intruded, with his prayer.

Indifference Day

And the day finally comes, as you knew it would:
Indifference Day.

Not a day for turkey or balloons,
but when you realise with quiet relief
that at last you are beyond hurting.

The careless sneer, the small barb,
that endless repetition has made large,
suddenly mean zilch. It's like
losing your faith. The taste is sweet and sour.
Energised, you throw off grief, and celebrate
this novel shift of power.

Those words of love, doled out on birthdays or
when sentimentally drunk, were just
another way to say *I want.*
You see it clear. It takes
a day or two for her
to realise there's nothing she can do.
And when the war is over, and
the bag is packed, you see
with pitiless eye, her separate misery.

Neighbours

I never felt hate before in my life,
but if I saw him out in the night
and I had a knife –

He's only gone and done it again,
put his bloody bin in front of my gate.
Though I never can catch him. See him grin.
Who me? You must be joking mate –

Get a life, he says. He laughs. *Stuff you!*
I'm getting a camera, maybe two.
Can't afford it, but what the hell.
And when there's proof I'm going to go
to the TV crew – then watch him yell.

I keep a vigil, night and day.
I see him leave in his fancy car,
and shortly after, her, his whore.
I'd like to smack her filthy mouth –
I never felt hate in my life before.

She called the police. I told them: wait –
I'm the bloody victim here!
They cautioned *me*. And him right there
with his bloody bin, and his bloody grin,
right by my bloody gate.

The copywriter

At the end of a long corridor, in a small room, they sat me down.
Sell this, they said, reverently placing The Thing on my desk.

We want green fields, contented cows, and springtime fragrance.
Give us hand-crafted, full-bodied flavour, satisfaction guaranteed,
in fifty hand-picked words, and do it by Friday lunchtime.
For the Client Cometh.

I stared at The Thing for a long time, there in the dark room,
with one grimy window looking out on the NCP multi-storey
       car park
where my panda waited among the jaguars.
And on Friday they returned.

The Client has Cometh, they said, *he sits and waits among*
the original Van Goghs in the Italian marble foyer, sipping
the finest French wine. What have you come up with?

I read: *Made from the pickled brains of dead babies*
and the sludge left over at the sewage farm, processed by robots
and packaged in a tin which costs more than the stuff inside,
to be sold at one hundred times its worth to the undead. Try some.

They stared at me for a long time, there in the dirty cell,
with the broken window looking out on the six lane highway
where no-one but the mighty dare venture.
Brilliant, they chuckled. *We'll sell millions.*

Colonialism

The slave,
black brown yellow white,
young old sick tired,
looked up from the
cotton rice rock dirt
and saw in the distance
the master,
fighting with another man.

The guard,
one of his own kind grown fat,
put down the whip and the foreign flag
in case they should send the wrong signals,
arranged the words in his head
that would sort things this way or that
and looked at the master, not the slave.

The slave
straightened his back,
washed his face,
moistened his lips,
ate a crust.

It would be nice to record he then rose up,
seized his chance, slew the guard
and with his brothers and sisters ran away.
but before he could even think of it

The master
on the same horse but different,
with the same gun but different,
with the same hard face, came riding back

And everything carried on as before.

Alter ego

She's not someone I would choose to be with,
God no! But she exists, persists.
Alongside the pillar of the community – me –
slouches this old slut.

She's like a friend from way back,
gone spectacularly astray.
Just when I think I've cracked it socially,
out she pops, plastered, spoiling things.

She puts her grimy hand in mine, holds tight,
drags me into doorways where
yellow lights scorch and noise explodes;
through slippery back alleys, forcing me
to sniff the world's muck.

I would like to get rid of her,
go about my honest business,
nod and smile and say the right words.
But she's always there, leaning against the wall
with that leering, sneering smile. Waiting for me.

No Bowl of Cherries

A casual look confirms
the world is essentially crap.
But out of the dung heap
the odd flower grows.

The infant life unfolds
in a sea of muck and vomit.
A nightmare of noise. Nonetheless,
a tiny hand curls like a tendril,
round your finger, heart.

Then that nettle bed, school, where joy
sulks its life away behind a cheap desk.
Even here, sometimes, a word
pushes through reluctant skin,
seeds a lifetime's pleasure.

For most of us, life is a dirty bargain,
freedom sold cheap in the market place,
made bearable by the occasional strong hand
reaching out to pull you through: the bond.
We're all in this together, mate.

Obeying orders

First they had to force my lips apart.
Clam tight they were; my eyes bulged
like those of a spooked horse,
focused on the Thing. They brayed –
they being the bigger boys, my waking nightmare.

Their grimed hands formed my mouth into
a Münch scream. They acted fast,
shoved in the yellow mass,
clamped hand on head, other under chin.
Eat it!

It moved in my mouth's cave,
against my recoiling tongue.
I imagined my tormentors' faces,
swollen, reddened, gleeful –
Eat it! Loving their sudden power.

No taste. Just the feel of it,
cold wet gristle moving fatly,
hating the warmth. Repelled by *me*.
Our small war, there in the field,
the faint echo of every war, when those
other, unspeakable things were done,
to the weak, the terrified.

My mind said: *Save yourself:*
if you do this, they will leave you be.
If you do this, they will be satisfied.
And nothing, in all your life to come
will ever be as hard. Eat it!

I almost believed, almost obeyed,
like a dumb soldier, following orders – yet
my body mutinied. Nausea triumphed.
I heaved, and there was the slug, free.
And there, running, crying, me.

The box in a box

They've made a new TV. It's got
a tiny screen, no more than five by three
– and I'm talking British inches, mate –
it goes inside your coffin, by your head,
fitted at eye level, just in case
in some way you can see things, when you're dead.

You wouldn't want to miss *The Street*,
Eastenders, or *The Bill*. And if
they put you in that box and underground,
you'll be dead narked when seven o'clock comes round
and you still need distracting. Look, it's ace,
there's fully automatic stereo sound.

The Pharaohs in their pyramids back then
made sure they took the lot: it won't cost much
to guarantee you'll always stay in touch.
It's battery-run, see here, you can
even change the channel with your tongue,
assuming you've still got one. Just in case,
it's switched on ready, tuned to Channel 3.
You'll watch the ads through all eternity.

The man who is out there

Drugged, drowned, strangled, which will it be
For my baby? The man who is out there
Whose name is Legion,
Is making the cage right now to keep her in.

Though he looks harmless, this man
Was the kind of boy who shoots cats.
Now, he keeps a knife and rope
In the boot of his flashy car.

In his time he has mugged old women,
Stuffed crap through the door
Of a quaking Pakistani. That's just
For starters. I saw him
In the paper, yesterday, head down
As they put him away for raping a child.

He'll be there again today, a different face.
He'll be behind the bushes, down the lane.
He's in the car, closing in,
The man with the over-friendly smile
Excuse me, darling, do you know the way?

On Gibbet Hill

It's still there. Same name,
but smarter now. A wide road
through ordered woods,
on the edge of a great city.

Someone told me – my mother? – that this
was where criminals met their end. Once,
only a granny or two ago, bodies
swung in the wind, heads bowed, like
naughty boys in the corner.
Eventually they fell apart. Jigsaws,
tweaked by crows. *They eat the eyes first.*

The house stood darkly back
from the traffic's whine,
surrounded by creaking trees.
Easy for the child's mind to glimpse
desperate men, haunting the gateway,
to catch their shrieks on the wind.
Like hide and seek. Grim playmates called
Come find us – we are not far away.

The name's still there. All that's left
of that iron-handed time.
Now Gibbet Hill's proud gateways tell
of men made good, in a safe world,
where no eyes see the dreary ends
of those whose disarray offends.
Above the dark trees, the crows
still circle.

Now what?

Just when you're hoping – even praying –
let this be the one to change your luck,
the one you can finally stop from straying,
the one that's more than a casual fuck –

Just when you're wearily rolling, smoking
the spliff you swear will do the trick,
or popping the last white pill, or calling
with the last excuse: *Can't make it, sick –*

And you can't, or won't, because of the trembling
leave the bed, and oh, the lights
still hurt, through the dirty windows stealing,
as you stare at the rented box in the night.

With a look that says he won't be returning,
the man has gone, and without a word
you turn to the wall though your heart is breaking
and try not to hear the voice in your head –

Then comes the knocking at your door –
will this be the one you're dying for?

A fly did it

One bite –
I didn't see it happen. I was
out there in the garden, drinking wine
at a friend's party.

The leg swelled up
like a sausage about to burst its skin.
It itched, I scratched, I bled.
The leg went strange.
I feared I might
have to have it off.

OK, I lied.
It wasn't a fly, it was a man.
It wasn't a bite, it was a kiss.
It wasn't my leg, but my heart that almost burst.

But the bit about having it off was true.

The winner

At last, my luck has changed.
For I have been selected from
everyone in my postcode, to win
a cash prize! Look, this letter here,
from Mr "Lucky" Break, of *Digest Which*
came through the door today to tell me so.

He sounds so nice. He says
I must watch for the post, because
there'll be a special notice, telling me
where and who to ring to stake my claim.

The envelope was marked *Priority*.
There's up to half a million to be won,
and my name's on a special winners' list
held by a notary in a locked safe
to make sure everything is truly fair.

I'll have to call a number. I've no phone
but Mrs Franks next door will lend me hers.
Meanwhile I am encouraged to think hard
on how I'll spend my win. A car,
conservatory, a long break in the sun.

I knew it would come one day. I thought
perhaps the Lottery, scratch cards, spot the ball.
Now this complete surprise. I'd no idea
they even knew my name at *Digest Which*.
You must have heard of *them* – oh, look –
here comes the postman now!

Holiday snaps

Nobody wants to hear about blue skies.

Give them tales of thunder, rain
honking down, pissing down, coming in buckets,
hailstones big as your fist: one killed a dog.
Lightning enough to rip the sky apart.

Blue skies are a bore. Like
someone else's happy holiday snaps.
Sod that suspiciously cloudless backdrop,
that unconvincing jaunty pose. Tell instead

how the thunderous row came,
ripping out of nowhere, fists flying,
wiping the smiles off their faces
as the tears came bucketing down.

The Old Bitch Bites

At night, the same warm spot
close to the fire. She worked, worked,
every day – except when the pups came.
Countless days, countless pups,
all sold, no questions asked,
cash in the farmer's hand.

Never ate much, a skinny dog;
table scraps in a metal bowl.
Hear it now, scraping the stone floor,
as tongue seeks out the last stain.

No vets. No need. She healed herself,
slunk to the barn, if kicked, if sick –
a great little bitch, till inexplicably
she bit his hand. His gun hand.

Stuff Science

Stuff it where
electrons wave goodbye
and quanta leap for joy.

Stuff it where
they look at the moon
instead of measuring it.

Stuff it where
genes are blue and
DNA means Do Not Assume.

Stuff it where
atoms don't split
but stay together
for the sake of the neutrons.

In-flight Disaster

We saw it first in the smiles
that didn't match the eyes,
as the beautiful girls went too often up
too often down.

We felt it in the tremor, heard it in
the pilot's reassuring voice.
Saw it in the face of one who
stood in his seat, looked wildly round,
was quelled. We heard the great
roar like the voice of God, saw the
sky tilt, fell through clouds on fire.

Terror rising in our throats, we
looked to heaven, as
the useless mask fell down.
Held one another's hands,
lovers, strangers. Gripped too tight to bear,
choked on half-remembered prayer,
mouthed our goodbyes, embraced, on this
eternal journey through the skies.

Four women wed

But on that night, that Hallowe'en,
a hex came down
upon their heads, their marriage beds.
And in due course,
the first bride turned into –

                    a horse.

Her husband was a farming man,
soon had her harnessed to his plough.
All through the muddied, earth-bound years
she dragged the day round, by his side,
his plodding creature, bridled bride.

The second turned into a dog.
Ran at her husband's booted heel,
his bitch, his slave, his Ariel;
obeying every curt command,
to sit, or fetch, or lick his hand –
no matter how he kicked, how cruel.

The third became a charming cat.
She walked alone, but sometimes sat
clever and clean, upon his lap,
and let his conjuring fingers lift
the purr from her, content with that.
His lovely, his familiar cat.

The fourth became a blossoming tree,
and in his house she stood so tall
she broke his roof, and broke as well
his jealous heart. He groaned, he swore
to cut her down, to break the spell,
then in her branches, saw and heard
a singing bird.

He stayed his hand,
and still she grew. The blossoms blew.
He searched for fruit and found it good,
so by and by, he grew content
to lie beneath her, looking to
the blest, the magical sky.

UFO

In aching loneliness the earth sits
like a plaintive aunt,
longing for a visit - anyone at all.
Surely, we say, there must be someone
something out there, with the grace to call?

No life on earth for a billion years.
Then suddenly the first bacterium appears,
a name in the visitor's book at last.

It might have come from outer space,
hitched a ride on a comet's tail,
stuck fast to an asteroid, who cares
as long as it's here. But what a bore,
sat there, silently vegetating.
And a billion more long years dragged past

Till the first mutating,
and something resembling mating.
That's life for you.
Nothing but waiting, waiting.

A couple of billion more years on
and life crawled out of the teeming sea,
which led to the mess that is you and me
and all the human fuss.

There must
be *something* else in that chilling sky.
But why? And what's to say,
that shy, elusive something may
know us, but *want* to stay away?

Did *you* visit your aunt today?

Generation gap

Arm yourself with all the steel you like,
you'll never be safe in this place.
This is *foreign*. Not the nice front
kept smart for casual callers. This
is the bit behind the main square,
those dark alleys that lead
to gut wrenching squalor.

You don't belong here, yet here you are,
trying to speak the language.
You find the words change overnight,
even the meaning of the words,
so what you say is not what you meant to say.
How to behave? Whoever makes the rules
it isn't you. Listen to
the sniggering at each silly slip.

Guide books won't help. They only tell
how you might have got through yesterday
when it was all different. Even
the maps have changed. You're lost.
You panic, make things worse.
Sensing your panic, they
close in. You are disarmed.

In praise of global warming

For some of us,
who have spent too long in the cold,
global warming sounds like a good idea.

There's no denying cold has charm
for those with the right clothing, attitude:
you know where you are with cold.
Nothing grows or changes.

But those who have endured the hoar frost,
reddening fingers swollen with an itch
that could never be sufficiently scratched; those
who have felt the chill seeping down to the bones,
icing over the heart; those
who have shivered too long outside the door –
we welcome the warmth.

It's the changes we're looking forward to.
New creatures will appear, not all of them desirable,
new plants thrive, ousting old favourites.
Some will see waters cover the land
they have fenced off, believing it their own.

They say the Antarctic will shrink,
but I have never felt the urge to go there.
They say we will lose the polar bear,
but I am looking forward to the tiger.

A red rag to a bull

That dress she wore: she was
asking for it. Up to here, and
what a colour. Blood red,
nails like bloody claws.

Those lips – mouth like a wound,
begging for it. Imagine
walking home alone, at night –
asking for it.
Would you let *your* daughter?

Then of course, it's *no no no* –
but we all know *no* means *know*.
That struggling and squealing was just a come-on.
Why was she dressed like that
if she wasn't gagging for it?

She fluttered, like a rag waving.
Can't blame me if the bull within saw red,
sniffed the wind, charged, pulled her down.

The Cold Shoulder

Inuits, long ago,
had a brisk way with the old.
When you were worth less
than you cost in seal meat,
out you went, and no bones about it.

Did Grandpa, like Captain Oates,
put a brave face on it, say
I may be gone some time –
and later, did the family
move the frozen corpse
away from the igloo, so the bears
could give him a decent send off?

Impossible to imagine
anything like that happening here.

Relationship

It looks solid, like industrial glass,
but you hesitate. You have
tried this before.

It looks as if
you could dance on it. You place
one foot, shyly, at the very edge
and press. It holds.

You step back and consider.

One step forward, then another,
you advance. Soon
you are feeling
confident, even reckless.
You try a few complicated manoeuvres,
losing concentration in the joy of the thing.

For at last you can do it! And it
is thrilling, certainly.
You pirouette, leap –
and that's when it happens.

Crack.

You are under the ice.

Joining the Women's Club

He thought that if he took the pills,
chopped a bit off here, added something there,
took gender counselling, he could join
the Women's Club.

He thought his snips and stitches
added up to childbirth's ripping terror;
that his little loss of flesh and blood
was equal to our bloody monthly flux.

But the members of this club
pay more than the price of a bottle of hormones.
And there's more to being female
than a padded bra and a wig.

Let him wear his oversized shoes,
pluck the whiskers from his chin,
call himself Carol till the cows come home.
This is one club you can't join
with bullshit and bonhomie.
You need your bollocks to be a woman.

Word association

The Director of Human Resources regarded me
as if I were an interesting species of rat.
Then said, apropos of nothing –
CHLOROPLAST

Quick as a flash I replied,
understanding the procedure well
DOUGHNUT

She seemed pleased. She offered
ZIMBABWE

I countered with the admittedly obvious
but perfectly innocuous
SPECTROMETER

But (without the slightest warning)
she suddenly shouted (the bitch!)
KITCHEN APPLIANCE

I was reduced to sobs – wouldn't you be? –
at the images those words evoked.
Imagine, coming straight out with it,
just like that. It was evil, evil. I could not speak.

When I calmed down, she said again –
KITCHEN APPLIANCE as if repetition
would somehow make the words acceptable.

And I saw through my tears, as sure
as honey grows on the potiphar tree,
my enemy sat behind that desk.

I whispered: *keep your rotten job,
if that's the way your mind works.*

The Tiger Mother

Surely, the most dangerous thing in the world to be
is a newborn tiger cub. Just think –
you're bite sized, tender, smelling of blood,
at the mercy of one who sees the world as lunch.
You've angered her by being born at all. It was
an inconvenience, dimly understood, a bloody
discomfort at the rear end.

How to ask for tenderness from such as she,
this weight of muscle, claws and teeth,
whose only fear is the bigger brute who fathered you,
and who definitely sees you as lunch?

Forget Blake, forget Rousseau, consider the tiger cub,
fighting for milk strong as brandy from teats
hidden in carpet stripes; scoured by a rasping tongue
that just might taste blood and, thoughtless,
chew off your little head.

How do any of them survive?
How did you, for that matter?

The way to the top

Learn the language, son
That's the way it's done –
Keep your words four-lettered.
Any punctuation? None.

Topics? Sex and dope,
Make it like a soap.
Simple sentence structure,
So near-literates can cope.

Plot line? Getting sloshed
Suits the great unwashed.
Lots of blood and tissue
When the heroine gets coshed.

Got to change your looks,
Live with tarts and crooks
To make yourself a writer
And to make it big in books.

Heredity

Down the broad track that leads to the tump
I walk in the steps of Iron Age women.
The farmer has hung a dead crow on the fence, like
a tattered warning flag:
we live by different rules here…

In the wild sky, too high to see,
a buzzard squeals, mimicking its prey.
Armoured in brambles, beyond the reach
of English Heritage, a standing stone
points the way back.

Not even the Romans dared
venture this far. The fecund track
closes in, claws at my legs; tears, stings –
I metamorphose as I walk. I am
suddenly in sandals, a robe, a cloak
coarse hair plaited down my back,
arms heavy with tin and amethyst,
alert for the threatening stranger.

The track dwindles. My feet tread it down;
I round the corner and there they are,
the family tribe, a thousand strong,
gathered together for the feast.
Generations deep, patiently waiting,
and by my side my beloved child
looking to me with forgiving eyes.

Optimist

I put the shameful thing in a box
in a drawer
in the chest
in the room I never go to,
and hoped it would die there.

Always the optimist,
waiting for the postman,
looking for the kiss –

The kiss that may come
from the lips of the man
with the key
to the box
in the drawer
in the chest
in the room I never go to.

To a Nightingale

I in my middle aged, middle brow, midnight life,
in my mid town second floor flat,
unable to sleep for the thoughts which muddy
my mundane mind, suddenly hear ...

Across the rooftops, distant, the thin wail
of a violin.

I get up, go to the curtainless window,
look out. See the square of light
in the dark town. And
the outline of a man, head bent,
bowing over and over the same phrase.
Over and over and over.

Indifferent to failure,
the banging on the walls,
the lateness of the hour,
the emptiness of his belly and his wallet.

Lost in the need to soar above
the compromising, muddled middleness of life,
and perfect a small miracle of sound.

In the beginning

Man said to woman:
I can offer you nothing but
blood, sweat, toil and tears.

The woman took the tears
and made a sad song out of them.
She took the sweat,
and made sweetness.
She took the toil, and found a purpose –
but she couldn't figure out
what the blood was for.

Said the man: you have the song,
the sweetness, the purpose – now
take the blood.
You can't have it all your own way.

This is the end of the line, here

Among the fly-blown charity shops
live the old, the weird, the drugged.
There are more people here with a screw loose
than anywhere else on earth.

Sometimes you can hardly fight
your way through the zimmers and sticks
on the ancient granite pavements where
they wait for death and pension day.

The young who have already gone too far
beg for the price of the next fix
under the statue of Davy, who
also got his kicks from chemicals,
but called it science.

So where do they come from? Not from here.
We have our bad boys, sure, our crazed,
our tarts, our hopeless drunks, our old.
But they're alive. Not these –

These undead drifted down from up the line,
hitched a car or train, were chucked out here.
This is as far as it goes. They wait,
nowhere to go from here but the sea.

Remarriage

Be one another's punishment,
whispered the dumped husband,
the abandoned wife,
condemned to be together, all
your miserable life.

Let hers be the face you have to see
on the morning pillow; his the breath
from the gaping, toothless, snoring mouth
until you part in death. Let him
cleave and her cling,
mistrusting everything.

Let promises you never kept
keep you nicely down and out,
ensure you always doubt –
for who can trust you now?
And who but one another want
that stained heart, that second hand vow?

At the conference

On day three, by mutual consent,
though the rules demanded otherwise,
we removed them. Plastic squares with safety pins,
worn on the right, defining us
Mrs, Mr, Ms, The Green Group.

It was Ted's idea (I think his name was Ted)
to shed some clothes. We were
by the ornamental lake, formulating theory.

We took a vote. Soon we were down to our pants,
each and every one in M & S.

Jan suggested skinny dipping, *To help us bond.*
Before we knew it, we were in the buff and in the lake,
having a whale of a time. Later we filed back on shore.

Peter began to peel off his skin.
No fuss, a corner at first, upper left arm.
It rolled off like faxpaper.
Surely it hurt?

One by one we followed suit. When we'd done
we found we were unacceptably red, even Rashid –
the colour of a final demand. So off came the flesh,
the muscle, fat. Now you could not tell
she from he, fat from fit, hunk from wimp.

We were ten skeletons in the sun, grinning our heads off.

Unlucky in love

One minute, Queen of Hearts, the next
her indoors, fit
only for fucking.

Soon, not even that.
See them in the street, those woman-girls
grown fat overnight, and sullen, pushing
second hand kids through
littered streets, to Boots.

Eyes dulled, hands red,
they yell four-lettered love
at children prematurely wise.
What made them so? Not Jack;
no dream of his, this
shuffled compromise. *She* then,
is she to blame?

Blame the trick of life, which shows
first the King and Queen and then
the Knave, time. He's the one who
salts the pack, says – *take a card!*

Plenty more where that came from

Glancing at the clock,
you can't believe the time.
Look where the hour hand's got to,
see how the seconds dissolve.
Surely it's running fast?
And the clock itself,
hasn't it changed somehow?
It looks so ridiculously *dated*.
That dark wood,
those Roman numerals,
the sad painted face.

Everyone else
has one of those smart silver jobs
controlled by a signal from somewhere else,
which never lose more than a
nanosecond a century.

You're stuck
with this miniature Big Ben.
How it chimes! So pompously –
as if time were something
it had any control over.

You can hear
the old cogs whirring. Out of date,
wrong as often as right.
Any minute now a bloody cuckoo will pop out.
You could write your name in the dust on it –
you have. Soon it'll stop altogether,
then you'll get some rest.

Bones

In West Penwith, redundant mine shafts
pock the landscape. Unfenced, unmarked, they lie
in wait for the unwary,
and the unwanted.

At the bottom of one such hole,
bones of drug dealer, crook,
a politician's 'mistake',
a rambler in the wrong place
and his dog, lie
in companionable tangle.

What do they find to say,
these unfortunate shades,
cast prematurely into hell? Do they
warily acknowledge one another,
like mismatched prisoners in a cell?

All of them have a shameful tale to tell –
except the rambler. His poor ghost
protests its innocence amongst that
sorry crew. The dog?
The most guilty of them all.

When he fell, claws scrabbling bloodily down,
barking, then whimpering, among those bones,
he – and who could blame him? –
kept himself alive awhile
by feeding on the hand that fed him.

The muse

Is with me now
but it won't last.

Like that louche, unsuitable man
who appears from nowhere
and liquefies you with a look,
he turned up unannounced.

Soon, embarrassingly soon,
we were at it together,
going like hammer and tongues
while he intruded into every orifice,
planting words I feared might grow
into something monstrous. He wore
me out, making me feel
sick in the pit of my stomach, yet
marvellously alive. Each day
I woke to find him inside me,
and I writhed on the end of the pen,
enjoying the rank smell, the taste and feel of it.

He's still around, just –
but, I know, too soon will come
the morning when he finds
a better hole to go to,
a fresh brain to mess with. And
all the fizzing fireworks of our few
short months together
will be over.

Suddenly I'll feel older,
uglier, fatter. I'll forget
to go to the hairdresser.
Remember to feed the cat.

she-mails

every day we boot up log on
mail our small triumphs
in unpoetic lowercase,
hi babe how ya doin guess wot –

subject: the muse,
words for windows to our souls.
We plucky, lucky women,
game at fifty, set and matched,
cd-romancing, laptop dancing
with the best.

intel inside, good as a man
and the Packard Bell still rings
when you're in pjs with fright wig hair
macintosh-dressed for laptop play
any time of night or day.

But this morning I logged on and saw:
u think your clever rite
well show u wot 4

Cutting to the bone

I am cutting deeper,
through pale skin, through yellow fat,
down to the mass beneath.

I have seen them in the French butcher's shop
slicing through well-hung flesh with blades
acid sharp, thin as paper. You could cut
your own throat with such a knife, hardly notice,
till the sting, the blood. And then
the desperate drumbeat of an outraged pulse
as life leaks away.

You out there, so fit, so fine,
so damned cocksure, have you
ever cut down to the bone,
and seen what lies there?

The sea at night

It crouches, heavy with threat,
so dark you hardly see the grey line
where earth meets sea meets sky.
Like some animal, the sea
always keeps one eye open.

That terrifying weight of water
leaning to the moon's pull,
covers the earth,
brooking no argument, hearing no plea
as it grinds out its gravelly song.

I stand on the edge, uncertain underfoot;
salty fingers strip the shingle from
beneath my feet, tipping me back.
The black sea approaches, retreats;
beckons, repels.

When I am dead
lay me in the cold earth, dearest,
a thorn at my head, rock at my feet.
I am for dry land.

You'll know him when you see him

So many people, for so long, have tried to tell
what he looks like. Is. But they agree
we'll get along just fine. A house afire.

They tell me he's an old guy. Then
a jealous lover, judge. Or not
a man at all. An it, a she.
He's father, friend:
he's there in the beginning, at the end;
creator and destroyer, love. The Lord Above.

All that, yet this chameleon's keen on me.
Wants me for his own, it seems, I am
the one that got away. Lost coin, lost lamb.
The hour draws close to our appointed date.
My God, I'm not prepared – how could I be?
Please wait for me, Please wait.

Failure

Failure stinks. He shuffles through town
in an Oxfam coat, shoes down at heel,
alone, of course.
At the Greasy Spoon, he's shoving in
the broken egg with chipped or smashed,
passing his time with the cracked unwashed.

No-one speaks to Failure, now,
because nobody ever cares to admit
they were intimate once.
They've dumped the tapes, the letters, snaps,
and if someone asks them *Didn't you know - ?*
they always cry: *Who me? No way!*
They see him come, they run, they hide.

But Failure remembers the wintry day
when he and they walked hand in hand.
He winks his eye when he sees them now
for he's pretty sure one day they'll stand
in sad reunion, by his side.

When the time comes

I can let go.
She won't have to prise *my* fingers off,
stamp on them, poke me with a stick.
She won't have to spell it out to me
as I once spelt it out:
this is the way it is, F – U.
It's all over, Ma, C – K,
thanks for everything,
though you could've done better.
O – F – F and out the door.
I can let go,
though it's a long way down.

Dead cat poem

She who flowed like mercury, or mist
over silent fields,
who had seen off foxes,
terrorized hedgerows, endangered
several species of rodent,
was now sitting on death's lap
and feeling his cold fingers.

We stood and looked for signs of her
in the grey bundle we had petted and stroked
lugged and loved through the years.
But she was looking elsewhere,
untidy for the first time,
dusty and in disarray.

Strange that when we buried her
beneath a flowering bush, in the sunny place
where she loved to sit,
we could not touch her.
Scooped her up with a spade.

Blood transfusion

This poem is anaemic.
It lies flat on the page, dull, pale
as a piece of veal, and
distinctly malodorous.

It needs beefing up.
I prod it with my pen, it does not stir. It wants
something stronger – lifeblood. Mine.

Stone faced, I search for a vein with my pen,
draw up blood, empty it over the words –
love, hate, death, birth, cruelty, tenderness
come dripping down.

Suddenly the poem,
now a dangerous shade of crimson,
takes on a life of its own,
slithers around like some demented slug.
It trembles, shakes, staining my
white shirt. I chicken out,
it senses my fear, turns –

It's coming for me! It's out to destroy!
I do the only thing possible.
I grab a pair of scissors
and cut and cut and cut.

It isn't for the sex

That's too simple. The thrill
of secret hand on skin, yes,
sly foot on foot, under the chair. Those
heat-seeking glances. And at night,
awake at five, belly on fire
as the mind logs on
to the body's need.

It isn't for the sex,
it's for what comes in its wake.
Senses in riot,
can't eat,
flesh falls away, eyes spark
consumptively. The mind's in
focus, though, filled with the thing
it wants, the thing in hand.

Acute awareness of skin. And beneath,
elemental yearning, not just in the heart and mind,
but in the very molecules
that make you what you are.

In the cell's heart there lies
the urgent helix, calling: *this* is the one,
my template's other half.
Join us!

The exile longs for home

He has been here so long, his crime
has faded from memory.
He knows he did something, many things perhaps.
He took the blame. But what, and where?
Something to do with love.
Someone, somewhere, loved.

It comes to him in dreams that he
willingly went away, put out his hands
to take the chains, willingly set foot
on this bare place. But in the light of day
he knows it can't be so.

And where *is* home, this place he looks so longingly for?
Such a hard going of it, he can't tell
where dream meets memory. Just as well.

For *home*, where place and people join
in glorious song, all that has gone.
Soon they will tell him this, and then
his punishment will begin.

I like the stone age best

Me and the other women,
squatting round a rough fire,
tearing the naked meat from the bone
with bloody hands. Then
grooming one another, picking
ticks, ticks, ticks from matted hair
as the clockless days crawl by.
Our brats, simian, mud-brown,
who knows which brat's which,
who cares? Some die.
We howl a day, then soon forget.
Always another, tugging at the breast.
And the best of it?
The elemental joy
when the men come back,
when the men come back with the kill.

Taken to the Cleaners

When you finally shuck him off,
wine-stained, grimed at the cuffs,
soiled from the business of
the grubby compromise of marriage –

When you can no longer bear
to be seen with him in the street,
to smell him, or feel him on your skin,
then do what you say you're going to do.
Take him to the cleaners.

See the experts strip away
those accumulations of fat
that make you retch. See
him pared down to the basic cloth;
scoured, boiled, soaked in alcohol
hung out to dry. Afterwards he'll look

Almost as good as new. Except
he won't be new. Look closer and
you'll see the wear and tear alright.
The faint shadow of an old stain.

Letting the anger out

I knew her dad.
When he caught you in the street,
he clutched your arm like the Ancient Mariner,
and out it poured.
Forty minutes we stood there, once,
while he told the tale I didn't want to hear.

He was drowning even then. A wiry man,
dumped overboard by his young wife,
clinging to custody of the girl.

The strain of holding on had drained
the energy from him. He told
of rows, and worse,
days and nights with silent child.
And when she did speak – *My God
the names she calls me!* It was
enough to make a sailor blush.

She's letting the anger out, I said.
The daughter blamed the dad. He was
too weird, too old, too thin, too poor.
No wonder the mother left.
His head hung with the weight of it.

He's sunk now, holed amidships.
I think of his anxious face, asking me
how it can be done,
the bringing up of girls.

This is a house where something died

Something died in this house.
You can smell it: a sour smell
seeping through floorboards and down chimneys.

You can feel it: the cold on you,
when you enter a room and the light goes out.

Whatever it was that died has gone long since.
But it left its mark here.
It certainly left its mark here.

What did it die of? Neglect, mostly.
A thousand small cuts to the heart,
the stubborn withholding of things needed.

It took a long time dying, but when it was gone
it wasn't really missed.

We wouldn't have known it was ever there
if we hadn't occasionally caught one another's eye,
smelt the smell of neglect,
sensed something not quite right,
felt the cold, and seen the light go out.

Christening

Choose a name, I dare you.
One of those famously lovely,
famously doomed women
will lend you theirs.

Diana, Catherine, Anne or Grace,
queens all, till the blade fell. And
Marilyn – who'd be a Marilyn now?

Err on the safe side, name her for a saint.
But most had the very devil of a death.
Walled up, chopped up, duffed up –
even the sinners had it tough. Who'd be
Jezebel or Salome, Myra, Rose?

Names once lovely enough to write a song for
raise a laugh now. Think Maudlin Maud.
Handles with a fine pedigree, fit for panto –
Gertrude, Agatha, Daisy Mae.

Name her Lucy for light, Sophie for brains,
Anna for Karenina –
and cross your fingers at the font.

Like I did. Like you will.

Half a million years ago
at the mouth of a cave,
a teenager stood
with a bone through her nose,
some furry fragment only just
covering her cave girl curves.
Like I did. Like you will.

Her mother stood where I stand now,
squarely in the cave's mouth,
and would not let her daughter go
out to the jungle nightclub.

Why? The mother knew, or thought she knew
there were dangerous predators there. Wolves,
ravenous old bears, rats, snakes,
who could unhinge their jaws
and swallow her daughter whole.
Out there, leaves and noxious liquors
were brewing in a pot that was actually someone's skull,
so that some unsuitable wretch
could slip the lot to her unsuspecting child
and steal her soul away.

The teenager in the cave's mouth
smeared mud in her hair,
narrowed her yellow eyes,
considered the jungle, sized up her mother,
weighed the sum of the things she knew
and the things her mother knew,
and decided the time was ripe
to make a break for it.

So, with a few choice words and a shove
she shoved off.
Like you will. Like I did.

Rolling in dead things

On the walk, the dog nosed out something dead.
She mired herself, rubbing
the rot well down into the fur. Head bent,
eyes closed, doing the job properly.

We caught her, shackled her to the lead.
She stood contrite while we chastised.
Later, in the yard, the same accepting stance
while we soaped and drenched her, scolding,
scrubbing at the stench.
She was left out to dry like a wet rug.

In Mexico, great packs of dogs
roam the shanties. You can see
every possible mutation of mutt.
No one scrubs, or scolds. The pack
seeks and kills its meat, scavenges, mates,
fights, and rolls in dead things.
It's what a dog does.

The Scientist

You couldn't resist it, could you?
You had to taste. And, oh, it looked
so very round and red.

You blamed me, but I
merely stood there, considering
the apple in my hand.

Scientists like you spend all their days
doing what Adam did,
nibbling at the tree of life
till all the world turns crab.

You stand on the edge, back to the garden,
washing your hands –
and every step you take is one step closer
to the angel and the flaming sword.

A car led the way

She followed the light,
stumbling, moaning. Found herself
a place behind some boxes, squatted down.

Room here at least, in the NCP, stalled
among these cold machines; like them
needing to be touched to life
by some more confident hand.

She was seen. People came and went.
Just another druggie, heap of vagrant rag.
Turn away quick, and go –
they couldn't know.

And when night came
in a wave of terror and pain,
her rite of passage, her nativity.
Just a child herself, but school
had taught her this: tell no-one, not
mother, teacher, welfare, friend.

She knew enough to cut him free,
fed him once, to still his cries,
wrapped him in a Tesco bag,
said her goodbyes. She took the lift,
whispered *my child, I am too young*
for this unwanted gift.